ABT

ACPL ITEM
DISCARDED

D1601465

No Sweat Projects
Bouncing
Science

by Jess Brallier
Illustrated by Bob Staake

Copyright © 2000 by Planet Dexter.
Illustrations copyright © 2000 by Bob Staake.
All rights reserved.

Written by Jess M. Brallier.
Designed by MKR Design/Pat Sweeney.
Cover design by Sammy Yuen and Pat Sweeney.

Published by Planet Dexter, a division of Penguin Putnam Books for Young Readers,
New York.
PLANET DEXTER and the PLANET DEXTER logo are registered trademarks of
Penguin Putnam Inc.
Printed in the United States. Published simultaneously in Canada.

Library of Congress Cataloging-in Publication Data is available.

ISBN 0-448-44088-1 (pb.) A B C D E F G H I J
ISBN 0-448-44096-2 (GB) A B C D E F G H I J

Many of the designations used by manufacturers and sellers to distinguish
their products are claimed as trademarks. Where those designations appear
in this book and Planet Dexter was aware of a trademark claim, the designations have been printed with initial capital letters.

And Now a Message from Our "Bouncy" Corporate Lawyer:

"Neither the Publisher nor the Author shall be liable for any
damage that may be caused or sustained as a result of conducting any of the activities in this book without specifically following instructions, conducting the activities without proper super-
vision, or ignoring the cautions contained in the book."

A Bouncer's Guide

ARRRGH!   Thud

Introduction

So why does this book exist?

- Need to do a science report or project?

- Looking for a subject that's really interesting *and* fun?

- Searching for an idea that'll impress your teacher *and* amaze your classmates?

- Need a subject that you know really well?

- Hoping to spend very little, or no, money?

- Are you running out of time?

This book is the answer to all those questions.

What this book will *not* do is *your* schoolwork. This book gives you ideas and illustrations you can copy, and it even helps get you started on your **research**. But *you* have to do *your* own work.

RESEARCH is gathering information for your project.

SCIENCE is the study and explaining of stuff that happens in nature.

So? What kind of science project do you need to do?

Reports and Projects Key

🐛 Oral Report

👦👧 Group Activity

✏️ Written Report

🖼️ Exhibit Project

As a student, you may be told to:

or ✏️ Write a two-page or a five-page report.

Present a three-minute oral report to the class. 🐛

or

Write a three-page report *and* present a three-minute oral report to the class. ✏️ 🐛

or

Write a three-page report *and* make a poster to be placed in the school cafeteria for parents' evening. ✏️ 🖼️

or

Work with three classmates to do a written ✏️ report *and* present something 🖼️ 👦👧 extra before the whole class.

or

Present an oral report and use stuff like handouts, posters, etc.

Luckily, **Bouncing Science** is perfect for any of these. As you use this book, it will tell you how ideas can be used for different types of reports and projects.

But Why "Balls"?

Because the ball can do for the science student what no other object can!

- Want to know why you bounce off an elephant whenever you run into one? Then bounce a small ball off a big thing.

- Want to know why a bear rolls up nice and snug to hibernate? Then crunch up a piece of paper into a ball.

- Want to understand how light reflects off smooth things and bumpy things? Then watch how a ball bounces off a smooth wall and a bumpy wall.

See that? The really neat thing about balls is that they are perfect models for understanding lots of different science ideas.

But of all the sciences—from astronomy* to zoology**—it is the science of physics which is best served by balls.

Astronomy is the science of the earth (a really big ball) and how it relates to all our neighbors in space. **Zoology** is the science of animals (which is why they call those places "zoos").

OK, OK, but there's a bit of science in most everything. Why "balls" for my science project?

Physics is the science of things—their energy and the way they move. And because balls bounce, spin, roll in any direction, and store and transfer energy, balls and physics are science's perfect couple.

You know balls. Right now, you're on a really big one. You also eat them with spaghetti. They help make your chairs swivel and your vacuum cleaner run. Some grown-ups hit, throw, catch, and autograph them for millions of dollars. But best of all, dogs bring them back to you for free.

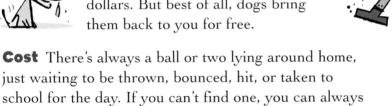

Cost There's always a ball or two lying around home, just waiting to be thrown, bounced, hit, or taken to school for the day. If you can't find one, you can always borrow a ball. **OK? So let's roll!**

Think Clearly: A Top Ten List

1 Before you do anything else, even before you go to the bathroom, **figure out what your project is.** Is it a group project? A written report? Two pages or five pages? Oral? Two minutes or five minutes?

2 **What do *you* have to do?** If you're working in a group, figure out what *you* have to do. (Even though it might not always seem like it, teachers know who the real slackers are in any group.)

3 Get started so you can get finished. Don't wait to start! You might get sick. You might get invited to a party. Stuff like this really happens.

Research: Allow five days, one hour every day.

Writing: For a **written** report ✏️ , write two hours the first day. On the second day, rewrite (make it better!) for one hour. Take the next day off. (You deserve it!) Rewrite for 30 minutes on the fourth day.

Practice: For an **oral** project 🎞️ , practice your presentation for three days. On the first day, practice it out loud behind closed doors once and once with a parent. On the second day, practice it once—with any changes from your parent—behind closed doors, once more for a parent, and one more time behind closed doors. On the third day, practice it one last time in private.

An **exhibit**  should be finished two days before it is due at school. Ask family members to check it out for you. Any problems with it? Tape coming off? Anything breaking? This leaves you one day to fix it.

4 **Check the spelling on** *everything.*

5 **Has somebody, like a family member, checked over** *everything?* Sometimes a different set of eyes sees stuff you don't.

6 **Is tomorrow the big day? Get a good night's rest.**

7 **Look one last time at your teacher's instructions.** Have you done *everything?*

8 **Pack the night before.** Is your exhibit big or fragile? Have you figured out a way to get it to school without wrecking it? Don't wait until the bus is outside honking its horn to figure out this packing stuff.

9 **If you can, pee before class.**

10 **Your contribution to this Top Ten List (whatever we forgot):**

_____

_____

_____

Getting Started
(The Amazing Note Card)

For as long as you are a student, you'll be doing school projects.

For every project you must do one thing: collect information. (This is also known as **research**) That's what a school project is all about: collecting information and presenting it to somebody. That somebody may be a teacher or other students.

So how do you collect all that information? With the amazing note card.

The Amazing Note Card

You can collect information about balls, for example, by **reading** a book (like this one), a magazine, or a newspaper; or **watching** a video or TV show; or **searching** the Internet; or **interviewing** somebody (see page 60).

Whenever you find something interesting on your topic, write it down on a note card. Be sure to write on the card where you found the information (for example, **Strike Three!: The Science Behind a Curve Ball**, a book by Lefty Dexter, school library). Keep creating these cards until you have a stack of them.

You've done all your research? Great! Now arrange the cards in some order that makes sense. For example, cards on the same topic should be together. One card should follow another for good reason.

Imagine that if you taped all the cards together like a string of cut-out dolls, you'd have a very rough first draft of a paper or presentation. **Neat, eh?**

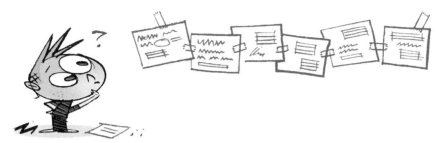

On the next 19 pages are about 50 note card-like pieces of information to get you started.

Read through some of them. Go ahead, right now. (We'll wait.)

See how they don't read like a normal book or paper? That's because these note cards are just the beginning of your work. They are not yet in an order that makes any sense. They're still like a bunch of letters (B, C, E, O, N, U) which have to be put in order so that they make up a word (BOUNCE).

For example, if you just copied these note cards out of the book and handed them to your teacher, the teacher would say something like, "That's a good start. **NOW FINISH IT!** Go write a paper that makes sense. These are just stones. Build a wall with them."

If this is a group project, think about how to share this note card work. By topic is a good way. Someone can research hitting a baseball. (How does energy go from the batter to the bat to the ball?) Someone else may research how ball experiments explain gravity. Someone else may find all the "extra" weird stuff on balls (the invention of bowling, why animals roll up into balls when sleeping, why golf balls have "dimples," etc.).

You can buy packs of note cards or cut paper into pieces about 3 inches high and 5 inches wide (use this paragraph's note card as a guide). Keep your note cards in a paper clip, or, if you do a lot of research, a rubber band will work.

Really Helpful Hint:

Once you have a lot of note cards, you should figure out what information is **really important**, what is **somewhat important**, and what is **not important at all**. So review all your note cards and mark those that contain really important information. For example, over the next few pages we've marked those note cards that contain the really important information with an **exclamation mark**:

OK?

And, hey, good luck with your note cards!

Sample Research

1 ‽ A ball is an object that is spherical. Spherical means a ball looks like a circle no matter how you look at it. Think about a music CD. If you look at it straight on, it's a circle. If you look at it at an angle, it's an oval. If you look at it from the edge, it's a straight line. Same thing with refrigerators and fishing poles—they change shape depending on how you look at them. But a ball always looks like a circle, no matter how you look at it.

2 ‽ Place a ball on a smooth floor. Poke it anywhere. It rolls, right? Nothing else does that. A pencil? (Try poking on the eraser tip.) A soda can laying on its side? (Try poking all sides of the can, including top and bottom.) Only a ball rolls smoothly in <u>all</u> directions.

3 Spin a coin around on its edge. Presto!—you have a ball shape, a circle in three dimensions. This means you can cut a slice through a ball anywhere and always get a circle. See for yourself. Have an ADULT (you've been WARNED!) cut slices through an orange or grapefruit. Then enjoy a well-rounded breakfast.

NOW THAT'S A MELON BALL!

4

A Super Ball dropped from 48 inches to a hard floor bounces back to 44 inches. A Ping-Pong ball bounces only 32 inches. Hey, what's going on?! The stuff that a ball's made of gets squeezed when the ball hits the floor. A ball then bounces when its squeezed stuff expands back to normal. The Super Ball has more squeezable stuff than the Ping-Pong ball, so it bounces higher.

5

Energy is the power that enables an action to happen. Every action—like a sound, you getting out of bed, a ball rolling across the floor, boilin water—requires energy.

6

Just before you drop a ball, it has potential energy (energy stored in a still object). As a ball falls it gains kinetic energy (energy that has to do with motion).

7 ❗

The earth has gravity, a force that attracts all things toward its center. The force of gravity is why you stick to the Earth instead of floating off into space. And gravity is why, when you hold up a ball and let go of it, it falls to the ground.

8

Weight is the measurement of gravity pulling on something. More gravity is pulling on an eight-pound bowling ball than on a four-pound bowling ball.

9

A weird thing about gravity is that it pulls a little less on a thing at the earth's equator than anywhere else on earth. A 150.8-pound ball on the North Pole is a 150-pound ball on the equator.

10 ❗ Think about a rubber ball. In how many ways can you describe it?

• What color is it? (Red?)
• How heavy is it? (Got a bathroom scale?)
• What's it smell like? (Please don't taste it!)
• How high and wide is it? (Two inches?)
• How much rubber is in it?

How much material an object contains is called its mass. Scientists like to know a thing's mass as much as they do its size, color, weight, and smell.

11 ❗

Momentum is the strength of an object's motion. That strength depends upon the object's mass and speed.

12 ❗

A ball has more momentum (strength) the <u>faster</u> it goes. If two baseballs of the <u>same mass</u> hit a window, the one going faster will hit the glass with <u>more force</u>.

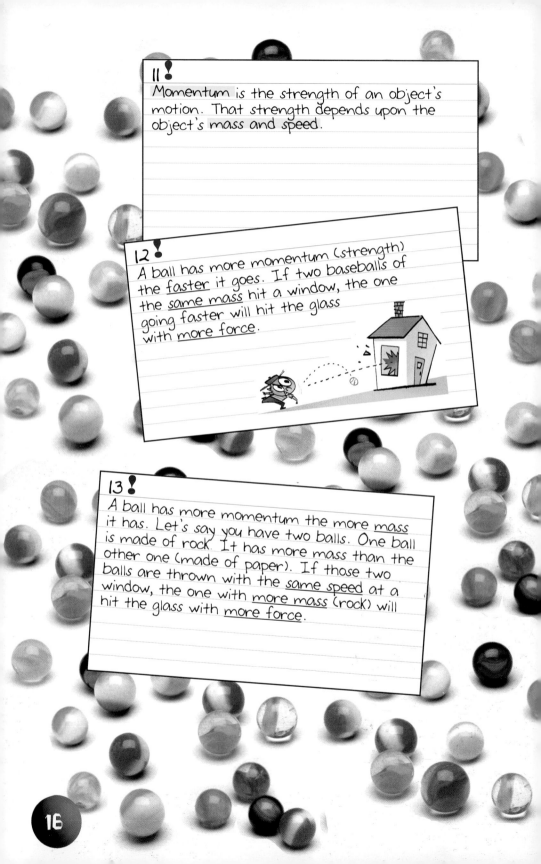

13 ❗

A ball has more momentum the more <u>mass</u> it has. Let's say you have two balls. One ball is made of rock. It has more mass than the other one (made of paper). If those two balls are thrown with the <u>same speed</u> at a window, the one with <u>more mass</u> (rock) will hit the glass with <u>more force</u>.

14!

Momentum can move from one object to another. For example, when a rolling marble hits a sitting marble, some of the first marble's momentum moves to the second marble. That's why the second marble moves. Or if your big brother pushes you, that's why you move. His momentum moved over to you.

15a!

Air and water slow things down. Hold out your hand and drop a baseball. Thud!—it hits the ground.

THUd!

KER SPLASH!

15b

Now go into a swimming pool and drop the baseball again. It takes longer for the baseball to hit the pool's bottom. That's because all of that water slows the ball. It's like you can run faster across an empty room than through a people-packed theater lobby.

15c

If you could go to a laboratory where scientists have big boxes with no air in them (a vacuum) and drop your ball yet again, it would fall really fast. That's because it doesn't have to fight its way through all the air.

16

A shot put is a metal ball that weighs 256 ounces (16 pounds). That's a really heavy ball. The world record for throwing one is almost 76 feet. A baseball weighs about 5 ounces. The world record for throwing a baseball is almost 446 feet.

ARRRGH!

Thud

17a

So why can't you throw a Ping-Pong ball as far as a baseball if you can throw a baseball much farther than a shot put? The Ping-Pong ball has so little mass that it can't gain enough momentum to overcome the air slowing it down and the gravity dragging it down. (Remember, momentum is mass plus speed.)

17b

And because of a shot put's large mass, it's impossible for a person to throw it with much speed. Without much speed, it has too little momentum to overcome gravity's pull. (Remember, momentum is mass plus speed.)

17C
A baseball has just the right amount of mass to be thrown fast. So it gathers enough momentum to go pretty far. (Remember, momentum is mass plus speed.)

18 One of the first people to figure out gravity was Galileo Galilei, an Italian scientist who lived about 350 years ago. Galileo (he goes by his first name) dropped two cannonballs of different sizes off the Leaning Tower of Pisa. They fell 180 feet to the ground at exactly the same speed and landed at exactly the same time. These falling balls were Galileo's proof that it doesn't matter how big objects are, they all fall at the same speed.

19

The smallest ball you're likely to see is the tip of every ball-point pen. Check it out. This tiny, hard metal ball rolls smoothly along as you write, moving ink from the pen to the paper.

20

What's the BIGGEST ball you'll ever touch? You're standing on it! (The Earth.)

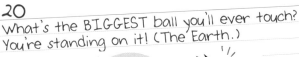

WHOA! MY FOOT CAN COVER HALF OF NEW YORK!

21

Shine a lamp on a wall. Try to find an object that always casts a curved shadow no matter how you hold it. A cheeseburger? A pizza? A baseball cap? None of them? How about a ball?

22a ❗ Most people used to think that the Earth was flat. But not ancient Egyptian astronomers. They had the Earth pegged as a ball thousands of years ago. When the Earth gets between the Sun and the Moon during a lunar eclipse, the Earth's shadow is seen on the Moon. The shadow is always curved. The astronomers knew that only a ball causes a curved shadow. Bingo! The earth is a ball.

22b

23 Sailors too had the Earth pegged as a ball centuries ago. Imagine ancient sailors watching a ship <u>depart</u> over the horizon. They first see an entire ship; then, after a bit, only some of the ship; then, no ship at all! What had happened? One answer was that the ship fell off the edge of a flat earth. Yet that ship would return. How could that be? Using cannonballs and little boat models, they figured it out—"We're riding around on a big ball!"

 It's a teensy weensy little ball!

Because the Earth is a huge ball, you can't see forever. Even on a clear day. However, the higher the point you look from, the farther out you'll see. That's why a ship's lookout is as far up the mast as possible.

25
Did you ever put "spin" on a ball to make it bounce or roll weirdly? This is called "slicing" a ball. Place a Ping-Pong ball on a hard surface, put your index finger on the top of the ball, and then quickly drag your finger down along the ball's side. The ball will scoot off in one direction but then turn around and come back.

26 Pitchers love them, batters hate them. It's the curve ball (also known as the "breaking" ball). A curve ball is thrown with a spin. As a spinning ball travels, it pushes air particles to one side of the ball. That causes the ball to move ("curve") in the opposite direction. Think of those funny cartoon and movie scenes in which a kid holds a huge fire hose, the water shoots out in one direction, and the kid goes flying in the opposite direction. That kid's like a curve ball.

27 When pushed air causes a spinning ball to change its direction, this is called the Magnus effect. (Gustav Magnus, 1802 to 1870, was the German scientist who discovered it.) The Magnus effect is what also causes golf, Ping-Pong, and tennis balls to swerve when they're hit with a slice.

28 The faster a thrown or hit ball spins, the more it curves.

29 A rougher ball surface makes for a larger Magnus force and better curve. Even though it's against the rules, this is why pitchers sometimes try to secretly rough up a baseball with their fingernails or hidden sandpaper.

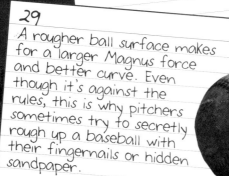

30 Tape a string to a golf ball. Tape the other end of the string to the top of a door frame. Make sure the ball doesn't touch the floor. You just made a pendulum. Pull the ball to the side about a foot and let go. It swings down, back up, back down, back up, down, up, and continues to do so. How many times does it swing? Does the length of the swing change?

31
When it comes to pendulums, what's going on?! It's all about gravity. When you first release the pendulum ball, it's pulled down by gravity, speeding up as it moves toward the floor. But as soon as the ball starts to swing back up, gravity pulls from the opposite direction, slowing the ball.

32 !
A moving ball is slowed by friction whenever the ball touches something else. That something else can be grass, a sandy beach, or air and water.

33! Friction is a force that resists motion when two things touch each other. Imagine life if moving things stopped only when they slammed into bigger things. Buses would go right past their stops. Your soccer ball would always end up in somebody else's yard. Thankfully, when things rub against other things, the motion creates friction. Friction works opposite the direction in which a moving thing is headed.

34! A special thing about any ball is that it touches the ground at only one small point. Set a book and a ball on the table. See how much of the book touches the table? See how little of the ball does? This tiny bit of touching cuts down on friction, which is another reason why balls are so great at rolling. Give the ball and the book each a good push. See?

35! Place a big book on the floor. Push it with one finger. Now put a few marbles under the book and push it again. The book moves more easily the second time, right? With the book only, all of its surface touches the floor. That creates a lot of friction. But with the marbles, hardly any of their surface touches the floor. That makes for a lot less friction. What you've just done is re-invented the ball bearing.

36 ❗

A ball bearing is made of several steel balls placed in a circular track. It reduces friction just like marbles between a book and a floor. In a ball bearing, the area of contact between the balls and the moving parts is very small, making the friction very low. Roller skates and skateboard wheels, bicycles, cars, and lots of machinery use ball bearings.

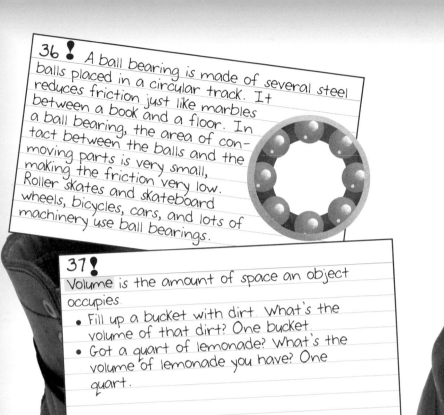

37 ❗

Volume is the amount of space an object occupies.

- Fill up a bucket with dirt. What's the volume of that dirt? One bucket.
- Got a quart of lemonade? What's the volume of lemonade you have? One quart.

38a ❗

Of all shapes, the ball uses the least surface area to contain a volume of something. Look at a quart of milk in a cardboard box. Now use your imagination. You would need less cardboard if you put that same volume of milk into a carton shaped like a ball.

38b

If you were in the business of selling milk, you could save a lot of money on cardboard if you put your milk in balls instead of in boxes. The problem is that your milk would always be rolling off store shelves or out of kitchen refrigerators.

39a

Hibernating bears curl up into balls to sleep through the winter. Think of the bear's skin as cardboard and everything in the cardboard skin as those parts of the bear that have to be kept warm. The less skin that is exposed, the less chance there is for the bear's body heat to escape. It takes less skin to enclose a bear who is curled in a circle than a bear who is completely stretched out.

39b

Don't you do that when you sleep? When it's cold, don't you curl up in a ball under a blanket? And when it's hot, don't you sleep with your arms and legs out wide?

40

Teapots are made so they are as much like balls as is possible. Heat is lost from a teapot through its outside surface. A ball-shaped teapot loses its heat much more slowly than a square-shaped teapot because it has less outside surface area.

41

An object's center of gravity is the point around which the object can be balanced. Try to balance a book, like this one, on the tip of your index finger. Did you do it? Almost? That spot on the book which touches the tip of your finger is the book's center of gravity. A ball's center of gravity is always at its exact center.

42 Line up four friends facing a smooth wall and give each a tennis ball. Have them throw the balls straight against the wall. All the balls bounce off in about the same way, right? This is how light bounces off of smooth things, like a mirror. When light bounces like this, it's called regular reflection.

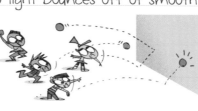

43 Line up your friends again. But this time have them throw the balls against a rough wall (a brick wall will do). This time each ball bounced off in a different direction, right? Light that bounces irregularly is diffuse reflection.

44 ❗
Centrifugal force causes spinning things to move outward, away from the center of their spin. What best demonstrates this scientific notion? A ball. Tie a string to a small ball. Spin the string and ball like a lasso. The spinning ball wants to move away from you. (Also see "Anti-Gravitational Balls" on pages 46 and 47.)

45! From the top of a door frame or a high table, hang a Ping-Pong ball from a string. With a drinking straw, blow on the hanging ball from below. Blow hard enough and the ball will happily stay, suspended, in the air stream. Hey, what's going on?! Air that's moving—like the air under the ball—is less forceful than still air. Objects in air hang out where the air is weakest. That's why a leaf rides on wind and an airplane rides on the air that moves under its wings.

46! Bounce a beach ball or basketball when it is fully inflated: BOING! Now let out most of the air and bounce it again: THUD! Hey, what's going on?! Air can be squeezed then resume its former volume. A ball bounces as all the air in it expands after being squeezed by the blow against the floor. A ball with little air in it has little to squeeze or expand—it can't bounce!

47

A hundred years ago, gyms were homes to nothing but boring push-ups and bar chinning. Until Dr. James Naismith invented an indoor game that required players to throw a ball into a hoop high on the wall. He called it "basketball."

48 ❗ When you throw a ball, it follows a curved path to the ground, right? This path is called projectile motion. The forces at work on the ball are those caused by your arm, air resistance (friction), maybe wind, and the one that always wins in the end no matter how strong your arm—gravity.

Getting Your Dexters in a Row
(Setting Your Priorities)

Well, What about Balls?

For your science project, are you going to present every bit of science that can be explained by balls? Or are you going to focus on energy transfer? Or gravity?

You've done some research by this point. What part of that information are you going to use? Or do you need to do more research?

Sample

Let's say you decided to focus your balls science project on gravity. Let's also say you like to play catch. Maybe a good title for your report would be "Gravity and Playing Catch."

Go back to the note cards. Although the ones in this book are only a sampling, pretend they are *all* your note cards. Now mark those—go ahead, use a pencil, put a little check mark (✔) on each one—that you would use to prepare a short oral report called "Gravity and Playing Catch."

To check your selection against ours, see page 64.

Organizing All the Information

Be very clear as to what your report is *about*. You do this by giving a title to your exhibit 🖼, or with the opening sentences of a paper 📄, or in the first few sentences of an oral report 🎬.

This will be helpful to your listeners and readers. But, better yet, a clear understanding of what you're working on will be of great help to *you*. Let's pretend your topic is "Gravity and Playing Catch." You might want to write that down on a piece of paper and keep it in front of you.

Remember, in a paper or oral report, first clearly write what your topic is. Follow that with the information you collected and selected. And at the very end, sum up your topic in a couple of sentences.

Really Helpful Hints:

- This is a science project. Do not use goofy humor or too much sports stuff as your main topic. At most, this funny info (also known as *trivia*) should be sprinkled in to pep up a report. A little goes a long way. Remember, your science teacher is looking for scientific information.

- Once you've picked the note cards from which you'll write your report, number them! Otherwise, gravity pulling them out of your hand (you drop them) might be a full-blown disaster.

- If you're doing an oral report and using note cards or sheets of paper, number them! That way, you won't worry about losing your place when you're in front of the class.

- If you will refer to a written paper during your oral report, make doing that as easy as possible. Print out the report in large, easy-to-read letters

LIKE THIS.

Experiments and Activities

Keeping Your Balls on Track

 Other than getting knocked on your butt by a bigger kid, "Keeping Your Balls on Track" is the perfect demonstration of how force moves from one object to another.

What you need.

- two straight pieces of wood, each about 12 inches long (you can use rulers)

- tape (transparent tape will do)

- five marbles, all of the same size

What you do.

Tape the wood, side by side, about half an inch apart, on a table or a smooth floor to make a marbles track. Be sure the table or floor is level so that the marbles do not roll by themselves. Experiment with balls running into each other. For example:

1 **Place two marbles on the track. Flick one at the other. What happened? The sitting marble stopped the shooter, right? But the momentum (see note card 14) of the shooter transferred to the sitter, making it roll.**

2 What happens if you do that again but hold the sitter? The sitter can't move so the shooter's momentum pushes itself back.

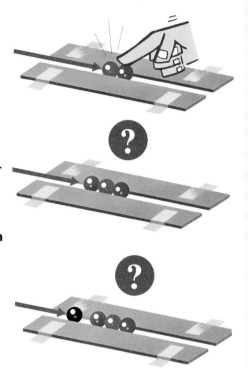

3 Set two marbles on the track so that they touch. Shoot a third marble into them. What happened? The shooting marble stops. But its momentum travels through the second ball and into the third ball making it roll. The momentum of the shooting marble is just enough to move one marble.

4 Line up three marbles so that they touch. Shoot them with a fourth marble. What happens?

5 Try other combinations. Try a larger marble. See if what you discover makes sense with what you've learned from your balls, momentum, and energy transfer research.

For a group project, the tasks to be shared include: getting the wood, tape, and marbles; building the short track; doing the various "flicking" activities; recording the results; and drawing helpful pictures of the experiment.

You can do "Keeping Your Balls on Track" at home and then write what happened. You might want to use the info on note cards like 11, 12, 13, 14, 32, and 33 to explain what happened.

"Keeping Your Balls on Track" is a great exhibit activity because it is so simple yet informative. On an exhibit table, set up a track and a small cup for marbles. Title the exhibit (like "Keeping Your Balls on Track"). Make a stack of cards. On one side of each card, suggest an activity (like "Set two marbles on the track so that they touch. Shoot a third marble into them."). On the back side of the card write "What Should Have Happened" and "Why".

The Great Ball Controversy of 1965

In 1965, the Detroit Tigers baseball team accused the Chicago White Sox of refrigerating their baseballs. Seriously!—the Tigers players said they could not hit balls that had been really cold as far as they could hit normal balls. And that must be why only 17 runs were scored during the five games played at Chicago (3.4 runs per game).

The White Sox not only denied cooling their balls, they turned around and accused the Tigers of cooking their baseballs. That's right!—the White Sox said when they played in Detroit, the balls there had been baked. The White Sox claimed that when cooked balls are hit, they go much farther than normal balls. And that must be why a whopping 59 runs were scored in their five games at Detroit (11.8 runs per game).

You be the umpire! Do cold balls have less bounce?

What you need.

- 2 to 5 baseballs
- a freezer

What you do.

1 Test the bounce of each ball. Note results.

2 Freeze the balls (in a freezer) for one hour.

3 Test the bounce of each ball as soon as it comes out of the freezer. Note results.

Were the baseball teams right? Could they really cool their hitting?

Imagine you're doing a report on the bounce of balls. Your report might include information on why balls bounce, why some bounce more than others, how bouncing with a "spin" works, and the difference in bounce depending on the surface. With "The Great Ball Controversy of 1965," you can also add information on how temperature may or may not change the bounce of a baseball. Create a chart. Across the top of it are two columns: "Normal" and "Frozen." Down the left side are rows labeled "Ball 1," "Ball 2," etc. Enter the bounce height for each, and report your observations.

For a simple and nifty exhibit, use that chart along with a poster board that includes a written explanation of what you did.

The Science of Bounce

How bouncy are the balls in your life?

Does the bounce of your balls differ depending on what surface your balls are being bounced against?

Check it out!

What you need.

- a variety of balls—for example, a rubber ball, Super Ball, tennis ball, basketball, volleyball, soccer ball

- yardstick

- pencil or felt pen

- paper

- different floors and surfaces(wood, cement, carpeted, stone, sand, water, brick, grass, etc.)

What you do.

Start with a smooth, hard floor and first discover the bounce of your different balls.

1 Hold the first ball at the top of the yardstick and drop it.

2 Mark on the yardstick how high the ball bounced. (It may take a couple of tries—that's OK—until you're able to see where the top of the bounce is.) Which ball bounces highest? Note your results.

3 Try the test again on different surfaces. Which produces more bounce—a vinyl floor or a wood floor? How about a fresh-cut lawn, concrete sidewalk, mattress, or gravel road?

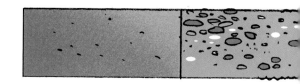

Imagine you're doing a report on the bounce of balls. Your report might include information on why balls bounce, why some bounce more than others, how bouncing with a "spin" works, and the difference in bounce depending on if the balls were heated or frozen. With "The Science of Bounce," you can also add information on how a surface may affect "bounce-ability."

To make a simple and cool exhibit, chart your "Science of Bounce" results and add a poster board explanation of what you did.

Water Balls

What's a good way to demonstrate how energy travels through stuff? With Water Balls!

What you need.

- two-inch-deep baking pan
- water
- 2 Ping-Pong balls

What you do.

1 Fill the pan with 1-1/2 inches of water.

2 Float a ball in the water at each end of the dish.

3 Push one of the balls beneath the surface of the water and release it.

4 Check out movement of the balls and the water's surface. You should see the submerged ball rise, waves moving toward the second ball, and the second ball rise and fall.

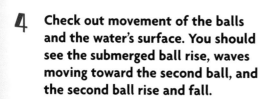

Hey, what's going on?! A wave—whether it's a water or light wave—transfers energy from one thing to another thing. Pushing the first ball moved energy from you to the ball. Then energy moved to the water touched by the ball. And now the energy is moving from one piece of water to the next, causing a wave that ends up moving the second ball.

For an oral report, this is a great activity to show your classmates and teacher how energy moves from one thing to another.

For a written report on the same subject, sketching the different steps of this experiment is a helpful addition.

For an exhibit, place the pan with water and a couple of Ping-Pong balls on a table along with a poster that explains what to do and the science behind what's happening.

Beach Bowling

If you wish to use balls to show the forces of both friction *and* gravity at work, Beach Bowling is perfect.

People play a lot of games on the beach. Frisbee, beach volleyball, and burying-hairy-old-men-in-the-sand are big favorites. But why no bowling? Can you figure that out? Roll a solid ball, like a baseball, on the following surfaces and check the appropriate "surface" boxes.

Surface	Suitable for Bowling	Not Suitable for Bowling
Hard, smooth floor (linoleum, tile, or wood)	_____	_____
Rug or carpet	_____	_____
Grass	_____	_____
Sandy beach (or sandbox)	_____	_____

The hard floor (like a lane in a bowling alley) is better than the floor of the beach, right? Hey, what's going on?! *Two things: the forces of gravity* and *friction*.

In the sand, a heavy ball is being pulled down into the sand by *the force of gravity*. (A lighter ball will sit on top of the sand.) And once that heavy ball is pulled into the sand by gravity, think about all the particles of sand touching it. Each particle of sand is causing *friction* that slows and stops the ball.

Beach Bowling is an activity that can be done in class as part of an oral report  . For an exhibit  , build a large box with several tracks in it, each track with a different surface (cardboard, carpet, sand). Behind the box, place a poster board with definitions of frictional and gravitational forces. Be sure to include a ball!

You might also consider making an exhibit  that compares a ball bearing (see note cards 35 and 36) to a heavy ball in the sand. You can get ball bearings at a hardware store.

Balls of Energy

Here balls do a nice job of demonstrating how energy changes but is never lost.

What you need.

- ruler
- 24-inch piece of string
- the heaviest book you can find
- two rubber balls or Super Balls of the same size
- two rubber bands

What you do.

1 Stick one end of the ruler into the book.

2 Lay the book on a table so the ruler sticks over the edge of the table.

3 Tie the center of the string around the end of the ruler.

4 Using the rubber bands, attach a ball to each end of the string.

5 The balls must hang at the same height, side by side.

6 Pull the balls away from each other and release them.

Do the balls hit and bounce away from each other until they finally stop moving? Hey, what's going on?!

As discovered in your research, energy is never lost or created, it only changes to another form. Just before the balls are released, they have *potential* energy.

As soon as they are released, they are moving because of *kinetic* energy. As they continue to bonk away at each other, that energy is changed into heat and sound energy. When all of the kinetic energy has been changed, the balls stop bouncing.

Show off your Balls of Energy in class or as an exhibit

Anti-Gravitational Balls

This is a fun addition to any oral report about gravity.

On a table place a large *plastic* jar (like a pickle or mayonnaise jar*) over a tennis ball. Move the jar with a rapid rotating motion until the ball leaves the table and moves up into the jar. Keep the jar rotating and you can lift the jar from the table with the ball inside.

Is this really a victory over gravity? Absolutely! Gravity wants to keep the ball on the table. But you're using *centrifugal* force (causes spinning things to move outward, away from the center of its spin) against *gravitational* force. When an object spins, centrifugal force wants to pull it outward. In this case, centrifugal beats gravitational.

*The I-Hate-Pickles-and-Mayonnaise! Issue.
You can try other jars large enough to accommodate a ball rolling around inside. Any jar with a mouth a little narrower than the sides of the jar will work.

What's neat is that in the same way, it's a fine balance of gravity and centrifugal force that keeps satellites in orbit.

 Anti-Gravitational Balls is also great for an exhibit. Place the ball and *plastic* jar on a table in front of a poster with a welcoming title like "Dueling Forces" or "Force-a-Mania!" On the poster include:

- instructions on what to do with the ball and jar

- definitions of "gravity" and "centrifugal force" (see "The Science of Balls: A Well-Rounded Chart" on pages 54 and 55)

- explanation of which force wins and why

The Science of Carnival Balls

Ever try to win one of those huge, stuffed bears or dinosaurs they have at carnivals? It's not easy, is it? Ever wonder why?

You can use the carnival theme for a fun, hands-on oral report  or exhibit project .

CARNIVAL BALLS

"Step right up, girls and boys. Three chances for a dollar! It's easy!" All you have to do is toss a softball into a bushel basket so it stays in. Easy, right? But no matter how gently you toss it, the ball always bounces out.

Hey, what's going on?! The basket is tilted toward you, its bottom curves up, and it's made of very springy wood. So when the ball hits the bottom—boing!—it's like a trampoline.

If you can bring a bushel basket and softball to class, this is good fun and a great lesson to learn before the next carnival comes to town.

The Milk Bottle Game

For this carnival thrill, you have to throw a ball and knock down three metal bottles stacked like a pyramid. It looks simple, but be warned: the bottles on the bottom are often weighted so they don't go down easily. Your best chance is to throw your ball at the point where the three bottles meet.

The Basketball Scam

Even Michael Jordan couldn't win a key chain at some of these basketball rigs. That's because some carnival operators tilt or loosen the rim a bit so that balls bounce off in wacky directions instead of banking into the hoop. Forget about bank shots—go for a swish every time. And keep an eye out for overinflated balls and undersized rims.

Ballmania

At the beginning or end of an oral presentation, it's sometimes fun to have your classmates goof off a little bit. Here are some quick and easy ideas.

HOW FAR CAN YOU. . .

- throw a Ping-Pong ball when there's no wind?
- throw a Ping-Pong ball INTO the wind from a window fan?
- throw a wadded-up ball of newspaper?
- throw a wadded-up ball of newspaper that's been soaked with water?

Hey, what's going on?! (See note cards 11, 12, 13, 16, and 17.)

GRAVITY AND REALLY BIG BALLS (THE EARTH AND THE MOON)

Look outside. See a building? It's there and not floating off into space because this planet's gravity is pulling on the building. Now, look at the Moon. It, too, is there and not flying far, far off into space because the Earth's gravity is pulling on it. Find this hard to imagine? Try this. Tape a piece of string, about five feet long, to a ball that's not too heavy—like a Wiffle or tennis ball. Hold the opposite end of the string and spin the ball around your body (like a lasso). Imagine you are the Earth, the ball is the Moon, and the string is the Earth's gravity. As long as you hold onto the string, the ball/Moon is forced to go around you/Earth in continual orbit. Does that help?

Oops!

Aristotle was a brilliant thinker who lived in Greece about 2,300 years ago. He thought he had proven that heavy things fall faster than light things when he dropped a rock and a feather and the rock hit the ground first.

Oops! He had overlooked a very simple balls experiment.

Hold up a sheet of paper and a tennis ball and drop them from the same height. The ball hit the floor first, right? That's what Aristotle did. But he should have kept going. Like this: crumple the paper into as small a ball as you can. Now, hold the paper ball and the tennis ball at the same height, and drop them. The balls land at the same time, right? Yet the paper's not any heavier, it's just a different shape. (The force most affecting a ball-ish piece of falling paper is gravity. However, a flat-shaped piece of paper is *also* affected by the trapped air under it that slows its fall.)

You just proved what Aristotle couldn't: that things fall at the same rate regardless of weight.

It's Supercharged!

Hold a Ping-Pong ball on top of a Super Ball. Drop them onto a hard surface so the two stay together on the way down. **PA-DOOOIIIINNNNGGG**!

Hey, what's going on?! As the two balls drop, the Super Ball picks up more momentum—because it has more mass—than the Ping-Pong ball (check out note cards 11 and 13). When they hit the floor together, the Super Ball's momentum transfers to the Ping-Pong ball and **PA-DOOOIIIINNNNGGG**!—it takes off!

The Big "Mo"

The key to success in many sports is how well a player transfers momentum. Ask your classmates to choose a sports activity that demonstrates the transfer of momentum. Examples might include the transfer of momentum among people, people and balls, or objects and balls. Throw out some key words like racket, kick, ball, blocking, bat, puck, foul, free throw, field goal, net, and so on.

For example:

- In basketball, when shooting a foul shot, momentum moves from the player's arm to the ball.

- In football, when one player blocks another player out of the way, momentum moves from the blocker to the opposing player.

Can your classmates think of others? Write their ideas on the chalkboard.

CAN TWO PIECES OF MATTER OCCUPY THE SAME SPACE AT THE SAME TIME?

Hmmm, wonder what some balls might tell us? Fill half of a clear, plastic drinking glass with water. Mark the top of the water with masking tape. Carefully add a marble. Then another. Then another. Now where's the top of the water? Higher up the glass, right?

Hey, what's going on?! Water and marbles are both examples of matter. (Matter is anything that has mass and takes up space.) Two pieces of matter cannot occupy the same space at the same time. When a marble is dropped into the glass, the water is pushed out of the way by the marbles.

Really Helpful Stuff!

These next four pages are here for you to use as you wish. That's right!—just go ahead and trace or photocopy these pages. You can then glue or tape them into a written presentation, copy and distribute them to your classmates, or attach them to a poster. It's up to you.

The Global Ball

Balls are so important that the word that represents them quickly joins any culture's language. If your class is *really* diversified, don't worry—here's how to say "ball" in 19 different languages (lang-gwij-is).

Chinese:	qíu (qui-u)
Czech:	miç (mitts)
Danish:	bold (boolt)
Dutch:	bol (bowl)
Finnish:	pallo (pah-lo)
French:	boule (boo-l)
Greek:	bvl (vol)
Hawaiian:	kinipopo (key-knee-poh-poh)
Hungarian:	golyÓ (gohl-yo)
Japanese:	tama (ta-ma)
Italian:	palla (paal-a)
Polish:	pilka (peel-ka)
Portuguese:	bala (bahl-a)
Romanian:	bila (beal-a)
Serbo-Croatian:	lopta (loh-ohp-ta)
Spanish:	bola (bowl-ah)
Swedish:	boll (bowl)
Turkish:	top (toap)
Welsh:	pel (peh-l)

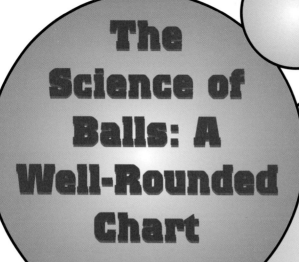

The Science of Balls: A Well-Rounded Chart

Gravity

The Earth's force that attracts all things toward its center. (Gravity is why when you hold up a ball and let go of it, it falls to the ground.)

Weight

The measurement of gravity pulling on something. (More gravity is pulling on an eight-pound bowling ball than on a two-ounce marble.)

Energy

The power that enables an action to happen. (Every action—like a sound, you getting out of bed, a ball rolling across the floor, boiling water—requires energy.)

Mass

How much matter (stuff!) an object contains. (Think of today's newspaper. Whether it's flat and unread, rolled tightly into a ball, or fluffed up to pack around something fragile, it still contains the same amount of newspaper. Regardless of its shape, it still has the same mass.)

Matter

Anything that has mass and takes up space. (Examples include water, a marble, you, and the Empire State Building.)

Momentum

The strength of an object's motion (like a thrown or rolling ball). The amount of strength depends upon the object's mass and speed. A ball has more momentum the faster it's thrown. (While a ball with more mass, rolling at the same speed as a ball with less mass, also has more momentum.)

Friction

A force that resists motion when two things touch each other. Friction works against the force of motion. (Ride a bicycle in deep, dry sand at the beach. It's not easy, is it? That's because of friction between the bike tires and all that sand.)

Centrifugal Force

The force that causes spinning things to move outward, away from the center of its spin. (Tie a string to a small ball. Spin the string and ball like a lasso. The spinning ball wants to move away from you.)

Yo! Spherical Rap!

Be sure to liven up any oral report with a little music and fresh lyrics.

Before you try to rap on balls
You would be wise
To use your eyes
To memorize
This list of words
That rhyme with ball
So you won't get stuck
Like we just did.

Aerosol	All	Awl	Alcohol
Atoll	Appall	Bawl	Befall
Brawl	Call	Catcall	Catchall
Caterwaul	Carryall	Cholesterol	Clairol
Coverall	Crawl	Disenthrall	DeGaulle
Doll	Drawl	Enthrall	Fall
Folderol	Forestall	Freefall	Firewall
Gall	Geritol	Hall	Haul
Install	Landfall	Loll	Lysol
Miscall	Moll	Maul	Montreal
Nepal	Nightfall	Overhaul	Overall
Pall	Paul	Pitfall	Parasol
Pratfall	Protocol	Rainfall	Recall
Seawall	Snowfall	Stonewall	Stall
Shawl	Scrawl	Senegal	Small
Sprawl	Squall	Tall	Trawl
Tylenol	Wall	Waterfall	Windfall
Wherewithal	Whitewall	Warhol	Y'all

Fun Stuff

When doing an oral presentation, it's sometimes a good idea to have fun with your listeners. Doing this actually helps them to pay attention.

This kind of material is really not right for a written report.

Following is some amusing and informative stuff to drop into an oral report on balls:

Since George Washington was the "Father of Our Country" that makes Mary Ball (George's mother) the "Grandmother of Our Country." Just imagine if George had used his mom's name instead of his dad's . . .

The capital of the United States would be Ball, D.C.

The Washington Monument would be the Ball Monument; and it would probably be much rounder.

It would be Seattle, Ball. And the nightly news people would say "Reporting tonight from Ball . . . "

Every town would have a Ball Street.

400 years ago in Mexico, the Aztecs played "Ollamalitzli," a game that closely resembled basketball. Now get a load of this: when a player put the ball through a stone ring, the spectators had to take off all their clothes and give them to the player.

As adults, what game did United States presidents George Washington, Thomas Jefferson, and John Adams play? Marbles!

WHY YES, I AM FROM BALL, LOUISIANA. HOW DID YOU KNOW?

TEE HEE

It looks like Ball, Louisiana, is the only town in America named simply "Ball." It is considered to be a well-rounded place.

It's always fun to bring ball-shaped snacks to school whenever the science of bounce is being studied. Spaghetti and meatballs or matzo balls are great, but a bit of a mess. So we suggest you go with —

POPCORN BALLS!

Ingredients

8 cups popped corn
1 cup sugar
1/2 cup molasses
1 tablespoon butter

1/4 cup water
2 teaspoon vinegar
1/4 teaspoon salt

Put corn into a large mixing bowl. Combine the sugar, molasses, water, vinegar, and salt in a deep saucepan. **ADULT REQUIRED!! DON'T EVEN THINK ABOUT GOING ANY FURTHER UNTIL YOU'VE GOT AN ADULT HELPING YOU!** Stir over low heat until sugar is almost dissolved. Cover; slowly bring to a boil. Remove cover. Boil rapidly, stirring constantly, for at least one minute, no more than two. Remove from heat and stir in butter. Pour in a fine stream over the popped corn, tossing constantly with a fork to coat all corn evenly. Grease hands lightly. Quickly shape into balls. Makes 8 to 12 balls.

Today's game of bowling comes from the ancient German game of Heidenwerfen (hi-den-were-fen) which means "knock down pagans."

There's a Ping-Pong ball in a hole. The hole is just a little bit bigger around than the ball. The hole is too deep and too skinny to put your arm into. There are no long sticks around. What can you do to get the ball out of the hole?*

*Answer: Add water to the hole and watch the ball float to the top.

Sometimes players of different ball games think they need more than practice to win a game. Here are some favorite ball-related superstitions:

Golf: Carry coins in your pockets.
Tennis: Don't wear yellow clothes.
Bowling: Don't change your clothes during a hot streak.
Basketball: Be the last player to shoot during warm-up.

Really Helpful Hint:

Go back to the note cards on pages 13 through 31. Did you find some of them—like cards 19, 20, and 47—more goofy than informative? These also can be used as a fun pause in your report. Ask if anyone knows what the smallest ball in the room is. Ask what's the biggest ball anybody in the room has ever touched. Sometimes when you're doing research, you just don't know how you'll end up using the stuff you discover.

"Well-Rounded" People to Interview

You will often learn more and have more fun interviewing people than you will doing any other type of research. When *you* actually interview people instead of reading books and magazines *about* those people, they are called *primary sources.* (Helpful Hint: teachers love it when you use primary sources.)

In discovering the world of balls and science, think about interviewing people who may work with, or have special knowledge of, balls. Like the following people:

mechanic (be sure to ask about ball bearings)
ball manufacturer (industrial or sports)
golf pro
tennis pro
physicist
juggler
magician

Additional Sources

Following are some of the books discovered while learning about balls and science. Most are available at your school or public library. You and a helpful librarian are likely to find other books that we missed. When searching the library, keep key words like the following in mind: "spheres," "circles," and "gravity."

Brown, Robert J. *333 More Science Tricks & Experiments*. Blue Ridge Summit, Pennsylvania: TAB Books, 1984.

DiSpezio, Michael, et al. *Science Insights*. Menlo Park, California: Addison-Wesley Publishing Company, 1997.

Guinness Media, Inc. *The Guinness Book of World Records*. New York: Bantam Books, 1998.

Murphy, Pat, et al. *The Science Explorer Out and About*. New York: Henry Holt and Company, 1997.

Nye, Bill. *Bill Nye the Science Guy's Big Blast of Science*. Reading, Massachusetts: Addison-Wesley Publishing Company, 1993.

Ontario Science Center. *Sportworks*. Reading, Massachusetts: Addison-Wesley Publishing Company, 1988.

Orii, Eiji. *Simple Science Experiments with Marbles*. Milwaukee, Wisconsin: Gareth Stevens Children's Books, 1989.

Parker, Steve. *The Marshall Cavendish Science Project Book of Mechanics*. London: William Collins Sons & Co., 1988.

Ross, Catherine Sheldrick. *Circles*. Reading, Massachusetts: Addison-Wesley Publishing Company, 1993.

Sutherland, Jason. *Curves, Sliders, and Sinkers*. New York: Random House, 1996.

VanCleave, Janice. *Gravity*. New York: John Wiley & Sons, 1993.

VanCleave, Janice. *201 Awesome, Magical, Bizarre, and Incredible Experiments*. New York: John Wiley & Sons, 1994.

Zubrowski, Bernie. *Raceways: Having Fun with Balls and Tracks*. New York: William Morrow and Company, 1985.

And while at the library . . .

Search beyond books. Check out the magazine, newspaper, video, and microfilm catalogs.

Internet

Search keywords such as:

acceleration

circles

energy

gravity

momentum

spheres

velocity

More No Sweat Projects!

Hairy Science

Hair-ily perfect for school science projects! With hair you can discover, experiment, and report on genetics (Will I be bald?), zoology (What do hair, feathers, and fur have in common?), evolution (Why do you take your head in for a haircut and not your foot or elbow?), and anatomy (What's the stuff made of?).

Shadowy Science

What are shadows? Why are they sometimes so big, sometimes so small, sometimes just the right size, and sometimes not there at all? How can shadows be used to tell time? Great fun and great science, the shadow is a winning solution for most any science project.

Thumbs Up Science

Confirming the notion that the human opposable thumb is as vital to the human race as is the brain, **Thumbs Up Science** guides the reader through scientific research, observation, and investigation. Along the way, the book provides a range of individual and group activities from thumb essentials (testing the opposable thumb and the secrets behind tendon-driven finger movements) to thumb fun (palmistry and thumb wrestling).

Suggestion Selection (see "Getting Your Dexters in a Row," page 32)

If we were preparing a report on "Gravity and Playing Catch," we would pull the following note cards out of those provided: 2, 4, 6, 7, 8, 11, 12, 13, 15-a, 17-a, 17-b, 17-c, and 18.